# Verses For Greeting Cards

*100 Rhyming Poems For Use In Card Making*

by

Helen M. Clarke

A little collection of verses
To help you – if help you should need
Embellish your cards with a message
In rhymes which are easy to read

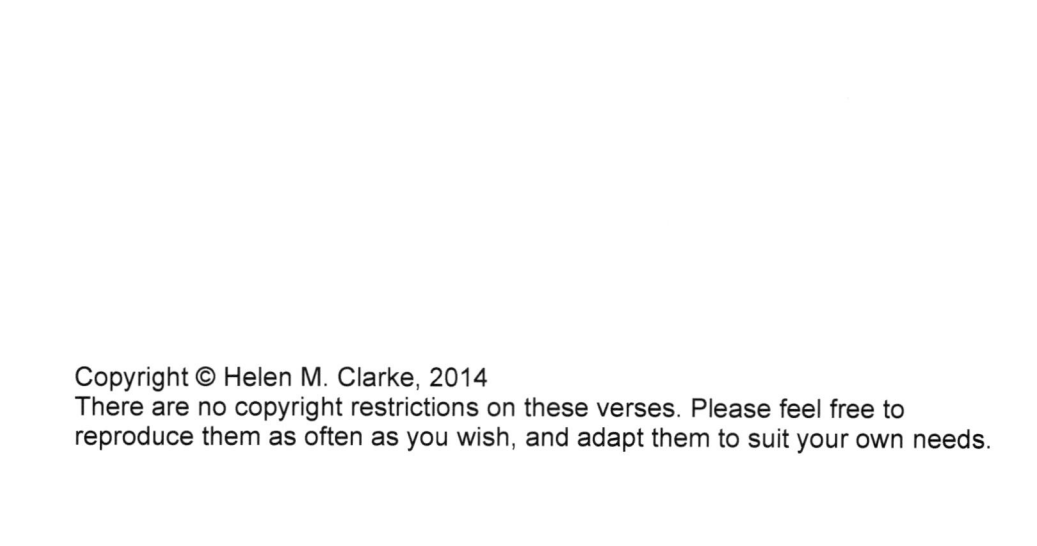

Copyright © Helen M. Clarke, 2014
There are no copyright restrictions on these verses. Please feel free to reproduce them as often as you wish, and adapt them to suit your own needs.

# Contents

1. Birthday General
2. Belated Birthday/Sorry It's Late
3. Milestone Birthdays
4. Family Birthday/Mother's Day/Father's Day
5. Special Friend
6. Engagement & Wedding
7. Wedding Anniversary
8. Get Well
9. Good Luck
10. Congratulations
11. Valentine
12. Leaving, Moving House & New Home
13. New Job & Retirement
14. New Baby
15. Thank You, Sorry & Keeping In Touch
16. Sympathy/Thinking Of You
17. Christmas
18. Easter & New Year
19. Christening/Baptism & Confirmation
20. For Children

# 1. Birthday General

*(1a)*
A special birthday greeting -
Best wishes! Here's to you!
Enjoy yourself, have lots of fun
Today and all year through

*(1b)*
A special birthday wish for you
For happiness and peace
For hopes to be fulfilled and
Life's rich blessings to increase

*(1c)*
A birthday should be magical
Like childhood ones gone by
So why not make a birthday wish?
It's surely worth a try
Allow yourself some dreaming time
And fantasise a while
- A birthday treat from *you* to *you*
To bring a little smile

*(1d)*
Another year older and wiser
A few more grey streaks in your hair
This age thing's no joke, but keep smiling
There's really no need to despair

*(1e)*
These birthdays keep on coming round
The years keep flying by
That extra candle on the cake
Can make the toughest cry
But think of all the wisdom gained
The skills, the common sense
And as for tales of olden days
Your repertoire's immense!

**(1f)**
Another birthday, more grey hairs
More furrows on your brow
More candles on your cake than
Health and Safety will allow
Your creaking knees have lost their spring
You're less dynamic too
This ageing thing's not funny
- Shame there's nothing you can do!

**(1g)**
Feeling old?
With wrinkled skin?
Hairs of grey?
And flabby chin?
Muscles stiff?
Waist like a tub?
Not much zip left?…
…Join the club!

**(1h)**
Another year older
But – hey, don't despair
You've still got your teeth
And you've still got your hair
Okay, you're less trendy
Less cool and less fit
Your street cred's in tatters
You're wilting a bit
But thousands of pleasures
Lie waiting ahead –
Like warm, cosy slippers
And cocoa in bed

**(1i)**
*Another* birthday? *Can't* be true!
Another year flown past?
But don't despair – you're not *that* old
It's just that time goes fast

# 2. Belated Birthday/Sorry It's Late

### *(2a)*
Although this greeting's rather late
It really is sincere
A wish for health and happiness
Throughout the coming year

### *(2b)*
I thought about your birthday
The card was all but signed
But when the crucial moment came
It kind of slipped my mind

### *(2c)*
I thought about your birthday
I focused on the date
Your card was all but posted then …
- Well, somehow, now it's late

### *(2d)*
I wasn't neglectful
Or caught on the hop
I wasn't too lazy
To go to the shop
I thought of your birthday
And programmed my brain
To give me good warning
But all was in vain
My system proved faulty
My mind went to pot
And – can you believe it?
I went and forgot!

# 3. Milestone Birthdays

### (3a) 18th Birthday
Well this is it! Eighteen at last
Your adult life's begun
Exciting options lie ahead
Enjoy your day, have fun

### (3b) 18th Birthday
Your eighteenth birthday! Here's to you!
You're really on your way
Make plans and dreams, have lots of fun
The future starts today

### (3c) Birthday Ending In 0
The truth is sometimes painful
And as the years go by
That sudden change from nine to nought
Can cause an anguished sigh
A glance towards the mirror
Sends shivers down your spine
'Those grooves and lines, those hairs of grey
Can they be truly mine?'
So focus on the good things
Like presents, cards and fun
And on your birthday, think of this –
Another decade's done!

### *(3d) 40th Birthday*

Add **eight** and **eight** together
Then add on **twenty-four**
Or, if you like, take **ten** and **ten**
Then double up the score
Or adding **twelve** and **sixteen**
With one more **twelve** would do
Or **nine** and **nine** would be okay
If joined by **twenty-two**
Or, if you like a challenge
Times **four** by (**five plus three**)
Then add on **one** and **five** and **two**
To see what it will be
And now about the answer –
It ought to ring a bell
But if it doesn't, good for you
Denial works quite well!


### *(3e) Special Birthday – Older Person*

You've seen your share of changing times
The good things and the bad
And known life's range of feelings
From the happy to the sad
You're loved by those around you
For your special caring touch
You've made the world a richer place
And still you give so much

# 4. Family Birthday/Mother's Day/ Father's Day

### (4a) Mum Birthday/Mother's Day
You've always been so good to me
So loving, kind and fair
So thoughtful, wise and sensitive
Mum, thanks for being there

### (4b) Mum Birthday/Mother's Day
You're always so loving and caring
Unselfish and sensitive too
Mum, how can I ever repay you
For all the kind things that you do?
You're thoughtful and so understanding
A wonderful Mum through and through
It's easy to take you for granted
But, Mum, I'm so grateful to you

### (4c) Mum Birthday
Today it's your birthday
So don't work too hard
Make sure you observe it some way
Enjoy feeling special
Relax and have fun
I love you, Mum. Have a great day

### (4d) Mum Mother's Day Teasing
You slave away, both night and day
And show no sign of cracking
Your halo's really shining, Mum
So keep it up – no slacking!

### (4e) Dad Birthday/Father's Day
I don't always think of your feelings
My deep respect tends not to show
But, Dad, though I don't often tell you
I love you - far more than you know


### (4f) Dad Father's Day
I tease you, Dad – you're such good fun
And yet I hope you know
I love you and look up to you
Far more than I can show
I'm grateful for the comfort
All your caring ways have brought
Your patience and encouragement
Your guidance and support
I have so much respect for you
And value what you say
Your wise remarks and sound advice
Still help me day by day


### (4g) Dad Birthday/Father's Day Teasing
You're not exactly Superman
James Bond you'll never be
Your jokes aren't always funny, but
You mean the world to me


### (4h) Dad Birthday/Father's Day Teasing
Brains and nous, a sense of fun
Patience, charm and looks to stun
These I get from Mum – but Dad
*You're* great too, so don't feel bad

### (4i) Dad Birthday Teasing

You're slowing down and cracking up
Your bones and muscles creak
Your wrinkled skin and thinning hair
Suggest you're past your peak
But what's another birthday?
Just enjoy it, feel no shame
'Cos when you're on the scrap heap, Dad
I'll love you just the same

### (4j) Husband/Wife

I really am lucky to have you
We laugh and have fun, talk things through
You're thoughtful and loving and caring
I'm so glad I'm married to you

### (4k) Husband/Wife Light-Hearted

Good-humoured, thoughtful, sensitive
Kind, generous and clever
But that's enough of me - truth is
I love you more than ever

### (4l) Brother/Sister

We've shared so many ups and downs
Hopes, dreams and heartache too
That even when we're far apart
I still feel close to you

### *(4m) Brother/Sister*
We shared so much while growing up
The good days and the bad
I have such happy memories
Of all the fun we've had
Those times together made us close
We knew each other well
And still we have a bond more deep
And strong than words can tell
And though we go our different ways
You're always there for me
Supportive, kind and caring –
And as special as can be

### *(4n) Brother/Sister Teasing*
You used to drive me crazy
In more ways than I can say
- Okay, so nothing's changed
But love you heaps. Enjoy your day!

### *(4o) Son/Daughter/Grandchild*
You grow more precious year by year
You really are a treasure
A constant source of pride and joy
To know you is a pleasure
(*or* To be with you's a pleasure)

### *(4p) Son/Daughter Teasing*
Okay, you had your moments
Like any other child
Of making life – well, *difficult*
And being rather wild
Of all your many antics
There isn't time to tell
But all in all, it must be said
You've turned out pretty well

***(4q) Grandparent(s)***
You fill my life with meaning
In a very special way
I love you and look up to you
And value what you say
You're wise and understanding
Kind and caring, full of fun
I've learned so much from hearing of
The different things you've done
I really do appreciate
The warmth and love you show
The time we spend together
Brings more joy than you can know

# 5. Special Friend

### *(5a) Someone Special*
Where would I be without you?
You listen and advise
You're there for me, through good and bad
So thoughtful, kind and wise

### *(5b) Someone Special Light-Hearted*
This greeting is meant for you only
- It's deep and sincere, by the way -
It comes with warmth, love and affection
To wish you a wonderful day

### *(5c) Special Friend*
I'm not sure where I'd be without
A special friend like you
You're thoughtful, wise and sensitive
In everything you do –
A helping hand, a listening ear
Kind words and caring ways
Support and comfort, sound advice
Encouragement and praise
Your friendship means so much to me
Far more than words can tell
And please remember – *any* time
I'm here for you as well

### *(5d) What Would I Do Without You?*

I have so much to thank you for
I don't know where to start
You're such a special person
With your warm and loving heart
I turn to you so often
If there's something on my mind
You're there for me, no matter what
Supportive, caring, kind
You understand and sympathise
You help, and talk things through
You're patient, wise and sensible
There's no one quite like you

# 6. Engagement & Wedding

### *(6a) Engagement*
You're ready to make a commitment
The depth of your feeling is clear
Life's best to a wonderful couple!
Your future together starts here

### *(6b) Wedding*
You're full of love, your hopes are high
You've made your feelings clear
And now it's time to make your vows
Your wedding day is here

### *(6c) Wedding*
Your wedding day! How wonderful!
Good luck! Good health! Three cheers!
Enjoy your day – and here's to many
*Many* happy years

# 7. Wedding Anniversary

### *(7a) Anniversary General*
You share life's daily ups and downs
And help each other through
You're such a special couple
All the best - three cheers for you!

### *(7b) Husband/Wife Anniversary*
Devoted, thoughtful, lots of fun
Kind, generous and clever –
You picked yourself a winner, love
And I'll be yours for ever

### *(7c) Husband/Wife Anniversary*
We have something special
I love you so much
Your caring devotion
Your warm, tender touch
Our shared life is precious
I value each day
You make me so happy
What more can I say?

### *(7d) Mum And Dad Anniversary*
You made a home together and
You've built a happy life
You're loving, caring parents
And devoted man and wife
That's why your anniversary
Is such a special date
You're wonderful to have around
Thanks, Mum and Dad. You're great

### (7e) Silver Wedding Anniversary
Your Silver Anniversary
Sincere congratulations!
Reflect on happy memories
Enjoy the celebrations

### (7f) Ruby Wedding Anniversary
Congratulations! Forty years
Of giving and of sharing
Of friendship and togetherness
Devotion, love and caring

### (7g) Golden Wedding
Your Golden Anniversary
How happy you must be
Your closeness and devoted love
Are clear for all to see
You've shared life's many ups and downs
Joys, sorrows, hopes and fears
Together, as a partnership
For fifty golden years

### (7h) Diamond Wedding Anniversary
Your Diamond Anniversary
How special! Here's to you!
Through sixty years your love has grown
And keeps on shining through

# 8. Get Well

### (8a)
So sad to hear you're feeling rough
And really not the best
Let's hope you'll soon be on the mend
Take care, make sure you rest

### (8b)
So sorry to hear that you're poorly
Relax. Take it easy. Don't fret
Be kind to yourself. Nothing's spoiling
These things take their time, don't forget

### (8c) *Light-Hearted*
A rumour's flying round that says
You're feeling really rotten
But jobs will wait, cheer up, take heart
You're absent, not forgotten

### (8d) *Teasing*
You're under the weather
And down in the dumps
Off-colour and weary
And full of the grumps
You're plagued by discomfort
And trite *Get Well* verse
But look on the bright side
- It won't get much worse!

# 9. Good Luck

### *(9a) General*
You're edgy and you're nervous
And you're under pressure too
But just stay calm and do your best
Good luck – and here's to you!

### *(9b) Interview*
Expect you're quite excited
But feeling nervous too
Just be yourself and do your best
Good luck - and here's to you!

### *(9c) Test*
Good luck – expect you're nervous
Stay calm and do your best
Here's hoping all goes well and that
You'll sail right through your test

# 10. Congratulations

### *(10a) Success*
Success! Congratulations!
You've done it! Knew you could!
Now have some fun and celebrate
You must be feeling good

### *(10b) Driving Test*
You've done it! You're a champion
A clever clogs! A star
You've learned to drive and passed your test
- Now all you need's a car!

### *(10c) Exam(s)*
You've studied hard and persevered
You've coped with all the stress
Now have some fun and celebrate
Your well-deserved success

# 11. Valentine

### *(11a)*
I love you more than words can say
My heart belongs to you
My one and only Valentine
I'm yours for keeps - it's true


### *(11b)*
I have to tell you how I feel –
Besotted, on a cloud
I'm in a spin, my heart is yours
Be mine! I'll make you proud
I never really understood
How deep my love could be
But you're my one true Valentine
There's no one else for me


### *(11c)*
I just had to tell you I'm smitten
Besotted and head over heels
I love you to bits, I'm enchanted
Can't tell you how blissful it feels

# 12. Leaving, Moving House & New Home

### *(12a) Leaving*
It really is sad that you're leaving
And people will miss you so much
Things won't be the same, that's for certain
But all the best - please keep in touch

### *(12b) Moving House*
You're on the move and under stress
No time to think or rest
But don't despair – you'll soon be
Feeling settled. All the best

### *(12c) New Home*
A fresh new home, a fresh new start
So many things to do
Here's hoping you'll be settled soon
Relaxed and happy too

### *(12d) New Home Light-Hearted*
Surrounded by chaos and clutter?
Can't move for the boxes and mess?
Exhausted, short-tempered and fretful?
So glad you're not feeling the stress!

# 13. New Job & Retirement

### *(13a) New Job*
Good luck! You have so much to offer
With hard work you're sure to go far
And people will quickly discover
How clever and gifted you are

### *(13b) Retirement*
A new phase of life is beginning
Have fun, there's so much you can do -
Adventures, chores, hobbies, new projects
- And plenty of time just for you

### *(13c) Retirement*
You're not on the scrap heap
Or put out to pasture
Your *Use By* date's still far away
So relish the freedom
Make time for your hobbies
Enjoy every precious new day

# 14. New Baby

### *(14a)*
A baby girl/boy! How wonderful
You must be so excited
How proud you must be feeling too
How happy, how delighted


### *(14b) Baby Boy*
A warm and heartfelt welcome
To your precious baby son
A gorgeous little boy who'll
Fill your world with joy and fun


### *(14c) Baby Girl*
A new baby girl! How delightful!
How happy and proud you must feel
A daughter to love and to cherish
She's precious. She's yours. And she's *real*!

# 15. Thank You, Sorry & Keeping In Touch

### *(15a) Thank You*
A big and heartfelt *Thank You*
Sincere in every way
Your kind and thoughtful gesture
Really brightened up the day


### *(15b) Sorry/Please Forgive Me*
I really am so sorry
My behaviour was the *worst*
I didn't give a thought to you
Just put *my* feelings first
I hate the way I've treated you
It wasn't done in spite
I've hurt you and I'm so ashamed
Please let me put things right


### *(15c) Keeping In Touch*
I felt I'd like to get in touch
And say hello to you
To tell you that you're in my thoughts
And send good wishes too

# 16. Sympathy/Thinking Of You

### *(16a) Sympathy*
You're going through a dreadful time
And must feel so alone
But please remember people care
Don't face things on your own


### *(16b) You're Not Alone*
If ever you need comfort
Or a sympathetic ear
Or just some quiet company
Please know that I am near
At *any* time, I'm here for you
Don't face things on your own
However bad you're feeling
Don't forget – you're not alone
My shoulder's good for crying on
My heart has room to spare
My arms were made for hugging
And I do sincerely care


### *(16c) Thinking Of You Religious*
Don't face things alone, friends are near you
Remember there's comfort in prayer
For God understands how you're feeling
Whenever you need Him, He's there

# 17. Christmas

### (17a)
Warm wishes at this special time
The festive season's here
And may the love, goodwill and peace
Of Christmas bring you cheer

### (17b)
Best wishes and warm festive greetings
This magical time of the year
And may the goodwill of the season
Of love, peace and joy bring you cheer

### (17c)
It's Christmas - rejoice in its message
Of hope for a world full of strife
Through love and goodwill, peace **can** flourish
And give richer meaning to life

### (17d) Religious
Best wishes at this festive time
Rejoice! The Saviour's here
And may your heart be filled with hope
And peace throughout the year

### (17e) Religious
It's Christmas! Have fun! Make it special
Rejoice in that baby so small
Who came to bring peace to the nations
God's Son - the best gift of them all

### (17f) Religious
The heart-warming message of Christmas
Shines through all the seasonal fun
- Love, peace and goodwill to all people
Revealed to the world in God's Son

# 18. Easter & New Year

### (18a) Easter Religious
Rejoice! The Lord is Risen!
He lives! He's conquered death!
Our sins have been forgiven
Let's give praise with every breath


### (18b) Easter Non-Religious
Happy Easter! Spring is here
New life is all around
Take heart, be filled with joy at all
The riches that abound


### (18c) New Year
The old year has ended
The new one's begun
Here's wishing you happiness
Health, peace and fun

# 19. Christening/Baptism & Confirmation

### *(19a) Baptism/Christening*
God bless you at this special time
And may your loving care
Equip your child to grow in faith
Through fellowship and prayer

### *(19b) Baptism/Christening*
A prayer for you this special time
That through your loving care
Your child will grow in faith and
Of God's presence be aware

### *(19c) Confirmation*
You've chosen to make a commitment
To God, through faith, worship and prayer
To serve Him and spread the good news
Of His love for the world we all share

# 20. For Children

### *(20a) Birthday General*
Hooray! It's your birthday!
Today you're a star
- A Great time to tell you
How special you are

### *(20b) Birthday Girl*
Cards! Presents! Excitement!
Your birthday's begun
Today you're a princess
So have lots of fun

### *(20c) Birthday Boy*
Today you're the hero
It's *your* special day
You're Man of the Match
Both at home and away

### *(20d) Birthday Daughter*
A special *Happy Birthday*
Hope your wishes all come true
You're such a lovely daughter and
We/I think the world of you

### *(20e) Birthday Son*
A great big *Happy Birthday*
To a very special son
Today you're a celebrity
Enjoy yourself! Have fun!

### *(20f) Christmas*
Cards and presents, decorations
Special treats galore
Carols, parties, fun and games
It's Christmas time once more!

### *(20g) Get Well*
You're feeling poorly – that's a shame
Let's hope this little letter
Will help to cheer you up and that
You'll soon be feeling better

### *(20h) Get Well/Injury*
You're hurting and unhappy
And as fed up as can be
But soon you'll feel much better
And be back to rights – you'll see

### *(20i) Well Done*
Well done! You're very clever
You've passed! It's really true!
You must be feeling happy
And excited. Good for you!

Printed in Great Britain
by Amazon